T0016224

People
Around
the
World

Life and Culture in

THE UNITED STATES

AND CANADA

D. E. DALY

PowerKiDS
press.

Published in 2021 by The Rosen Publishing Group, Inc.
29 East 21st Street, New York, NY 10010

First Edition

Editor: Siyavush Saidian
Book Design: Seth Hughes

Photo Credits: Cover Cyril Charpin/Shutterstock.com; p. 5 Rainer Lesniewski/Shutterstock.com; p. 7 Esemono/Wikimedia Commons; p. 8 Dan Breckwoldt/Shutterstock.com; p. 9 sirtravelalot/Shutterstock.com; p. 10 (top) © istockphoto/fuchs-photography; p. 10 (bottom) © istockphoto/S. Greg Panosian; p. 11 Geo Swan/Wikimedia Commons; p. 14 © istockphoto/THEPALMER; p. 16 © istockphoto/bakerjarvis; p. 17 © istockphoto/Sean Pavone; p. 18 (top) © istockphoto/CarpathianPrince; p. 18 (bottom) © istockphoto/ChristiLaLiberte; p. 19 Delpixel/Shutterstock.com; p. 21 Artaxerxes/Wikimedia Commons; p. 23 (top) Bettmann/Getty Images; p. 23 (bottom) Raymond Boyd/Michael Ochs Archives/Getty Images; p. 24 (top) © istockphoto/LauriPatterson; p. 24 (bottom) © istockphoto/nndanko; p. 25 © istockphoto/RiverNorthPhotography; p. 27 © istockphoto/Beboy_ltd; p. 28 (left) © istockphoto/RyersonClark; p. 28 (right) Erika Goldring/Getty Images Entertainment/Getty Images; p. 30 (top) © istockphoto/NoDerog; p. 30 (bottom) © istockphoto/AvailableLight; P. 31 Noam Armonn/Shutterstock.com; p. 33 Yarnalgo/Wikimedia Commons; p. 34 Olga Bogatyrenko/Shutterstock.com; p. 35 (left) klarka0608/Shutterstock.com; p. 35 (right) Bruce Bennett/Getty Images; p. 36 (top) mTaira/Shutterstock.com; p. 36 (bottom) Mike Powell/Getty Images Sport/Getty Images; p. 40 © istockphoto/cnicbc; p. 41 Hulton Archive/Handout/Moviepix/Getty Images; p. 42 (left) logoboom/Shutterstock.com; p. 42 (right) Sociopath987/Shutterstock.com; p. 44 David Hume Kennerly/Getty Images Entertainment/Getty Images; p. 45 Robie Online/Shutterstock.com.

Cataloging-in-Publication Data

Names: Daly, D. E.
Title: Life and culture in the United States and Canada / D. E. Daly.
Description: New York : PowerKids Press, 2021. | Series: People around the world | Includes glossary and index.
Identifiers: ISBN 9781725321526 (pbk.) | ISBN 9781725321540 (library bound) | ISBN 9781725321533 (6 pack) | ISBN 9781725321557 (ebook)
Subjects: LCSH: North America–Juvenile literature. | North America–Social life and customs–Juvenile literature. | North America–Social conditions–Juvenile literature.
Classification: LCC E38.5 D35 2020 | DDC 917–dc23

Manufactured in the United States of America

CPSIA Compliance Information: Batch #CSPK20: For Further Information contact Rosen Publishing, New York, New York at 1-800-237-9932

Find us on

Contents

Introduction
THE UNITED STATES AND CANADA

Two of the largest countries in the world sit side by side: Canada, the second-largest country in the world, is the northern neighbor of the third-largest country, the United States of America.

Although it's larger in terms of land, Canada's population of 36 million people is far lower than the United States' 330 million total. Canada's population is lower, even, than the 39 million people living in just the U.S. state of California. Canada includes icy northern territories where few people reside. In fact, 90 percent of Canada's population lives within 100 miles (160.9 km) of the U.S. border.

Because these countries are so geographically close, it's unsurprising that their cultures—though different in many ways—share a lot of common ground. **Indigenous** peoples lived

indigenous: Describing groups that are native to a particular region.

The United States and Canada share the longest international land boundary in the world. Though they're distinct countries, this closeness has led to many cultural aspects in common.

in North America for thousands of years before European exploration, and their beliefs, practices, and languages remain strong in both countries. However, both the United States and Canada have historically been considered **immigrant** countries. Their current governments, institutions, primary spoken languages, and majority population were largely established and expanded by immigrants and their descendants. Both countries' cultures are colored by the coexistence and blending of different peoples, from immigrants searching for freedom and upward mobility in a "New World" to Africans forcibly brought to North America by the slave trade to those who lived on the land originally.

1 INDIGENOUS PEOPLE AND LANGUAGES

The top three languages spoken in the United States and Canada today are English, Spanish, and French. Before 1500, the indigenous peoples living north of present-day Mexico spoke at least 300 languages. Exactly how many indigenous languages existed, or whether some should be considered **dialects** instead of full languages, may forever be a mystery. About half of these languages are believed to be extinct, and many that still exist have only a few speakers. No single feature is shared by all these languages. They are **diverse**, and so were the ways of life of their speakers.

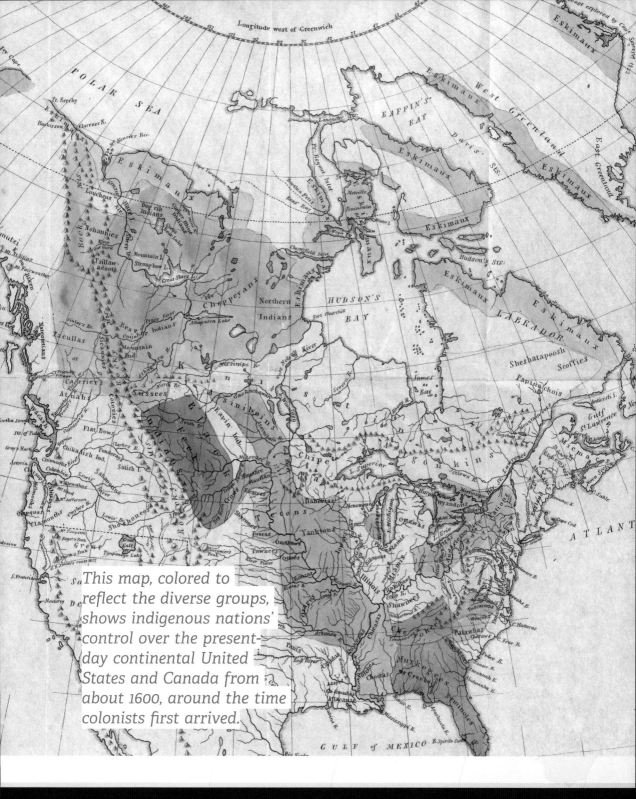

This map, colored to reflect the diverse groups, shows indigenous nations' control over the present-day continental United States and Canada from about 1600, around the time colonists first arrived.

diverse: Different or varied.

All indigenous peoples lived off the land, but the regions in which each group lived were wildly different. The Iroquois of the Great Lakes region were farmers and hunters. Some of the Great Plains peoples, such as the Sioux, followed the bison herds, using all parts of the animal to make food, clothing, and shelter and even carving dice and toys from its bones. People of the Northwest Coast became skilled fishermen, preserving fish with drying and smoking techniques. In the Southwest, almost every Navajo family kept sheep.

Totem poles, which are carefully constructed by painting and carving large logs, are important cultural monuments for peoples of the Pacific Northwest of both the United States and Canada.

The Right Name to Use

The term "indigenous people" refers to any culture that lived in a place first—typically meaning before explorers **colonized** their lands. Christopher Columbus never set foot in North America, but his mistaken term "Indian"—linking indigenous Caribbean peoples with the Indian Ocean he was trying to find—was long used for indigenous people. Many indigenous people prefer to identify themselves by tribe or group, but the older terms "American Indian" and "Native American" are both widely used in the United States. However, these terms generally don't include native Hawaiians and Alaskan natives.

In Canada, the preferred term is "First Nations," but as the Inuit—people native to Arctic Canada—are a distinct group, "First Peoples" or "Aboriginal Peoples" are sometimes used more comprehensively.

*The Inuit are indigenous peoples who occupy the northern regions of Canada and the greater Arctic region. They have preserved much of their traditional way of life to survive the **tundra** climate.*

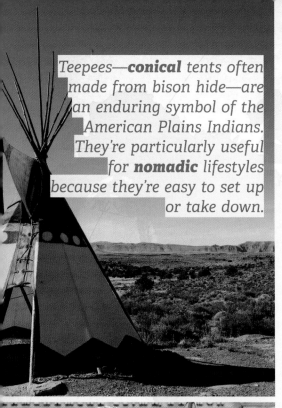

*Teepees—**conical** tents often made from bison hide—are an enduring symbol of the American Plains Indians. They're particularly useful for **nomadic** lifestyles because they're easy to set up or take down.*

This Honolulu statue commemorates Hawaii's greatest king, Kamehameha, who in 1810 united the Hawaiian Islands into a single royal kingdom. On the Hawaiian holiday Kamehameha Day, his statue is draped with flower lei.

The history of European settlers encountering Native American and First Nations peoples is one of violent conquest. While trade and cooperation between these groups did occur, so too did enslavement and warfare, the latter on a far greater scale. European diseases such as smallpox particularly devastated the indigenous population. Initial treaties were broken as both the U.S. and Canadian governments expanded westward in the 1800s, stealing land from indigenous peoples.

Both the United States and Canada spent centuries forcing indigenous peoples to adopt Christian beliefs and the English language. These changes partially destroyed indigenous traditions and culture. As part of these conversion efforts, some indigenous children were forced to leave their families and attend boarding schools. The governments believed educating children at these schools would encourage **assimilation** to nonnative culture. Today, the United States and Canada

This study period at a Roman Catholic Indian residential school in the Northwest Territories of Canada shows the experience of indigenous students at government-run boarding schools. Note the students weren't allowed to wear their cultures' traditional clothing.

Lasting Words

Indigenous languages loaned a great deal to the English language and contributed greatly to maps of the United States and Canada. The very name "Canada" came from *kanata*, an Iroquois word for village.

The names for states Illinois and Kansas, the city Miami, Lake Erie, and the Missouri River all came from native languages, along with endless other place names across the United States. Many names of native North American animals—which were new to English speakers— were adopted directly into the language. The names "skunk," "chipmunk," "raccoon," "moose," "caribou," and surprisingly, "woodchuck," became a part of everyday English, with spellings that reflected how the original Native American word sounded to Europeans.

acknowledge the wrongs of the past, but they can't undo the damage. Large areas of land—called reservations in the United States and reserves in Canada—have been set aside to give Native American and First Nations people back a fraction of their original territories. The preservation of surviving culture is an ongoing effort in many indigenous communities.

2 THE ROOTS OF TWO NATIONS

Culture emerges out of history and tradition. The 16th- and 17th-century race to colonize North America was a struggle for empire between all the major powers of Europe. New Spain, New France, and New Amsterdam no longer exist on any modern map. "New England," however, is still used to refer to six states in the northeastern United States, and English is the primary spoken language in both the United States and Canada.

CULTURAL CONNECTIONS

Canada has both English and French as equal official languages. Although the U.S. government operates using English, the country has no official language; all are equal under federal law.

In 1776, Britain controlled 20 colonies, including formerly French Quebec, when

The Declaration of Independence, issued on July 4, 1776, is a founding document of American culture and continues to impact the culture of the United States today.

13 North American colonies declared independence and became the early United States. Though the United States broke away from Britain, the U.S. Founding Fathers borrowed a great deal directly from Europe when creating a new government.

Early on, the United States built its economy on slave labor. Africans were forced to work on plantations across the young country, and the cash crops grown on these farms—especially in the South—made many white Americans rich. The thriving economy allowed political leaders to look toward the future. As the country expanded westward over the next half-century, it absorbed territories and settlers from other nations.

CULTURAL CONNECTIONS

It's likely that no long-distance **migration** in history has claimed more human lives than the transatlantic slave trade. Nearly 400,000 Africans were brought to the United States as slaves, and about 3,000 were brought to Canada.

The Québécois and the Acadians

New France included the colonies of Canada, which occupied modern-day Quebec, and Acadia, today's Nova Scotia. Geographically separate, French settlers in each colony developed different cultures: Québécois and Acadian.

Acadia switched between British and French control nine times in less than 100 years. In 1755, the British forced more than 6,000 Acadians out. Many displaced Acadians eventually resettled in the area of the present-day state of Louisiana. They became known as Cajuns, and their food, traditions, music, French dialect, and "Cajun English" became a key part of Louisiana culture.

Britain also gained control of Quebec, but they let the French-Catholic Québécois retain religious freedom and their own laws, which helped keep the province loyal during the American Revolution.

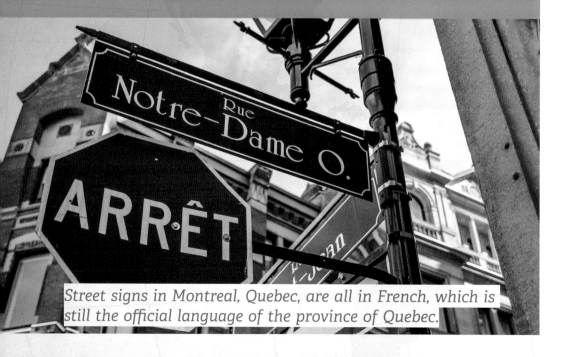

Street signs in Montreal, Quebec, are all in French, which is still the official language of the province of Quebec.

Spanish colonial architecture has influenced styles in Florida, California, and the Southwest. Puerto Rico—not a state, but a territory of the United States since 1898—remains mostly Spanish speaking. "Creole," meaning "mixed," is a term referring to the people of Louisiana before it was purchased from France and includes people from a mix of French, Spanish, Native American, Caribbean, or African heritage.

Saint Augustine, Florida, established by the Spanish in 1565, is the oldest permanent and continuously inhabited settlement in the United States. The city still features Spanish colonial architecture.

Tejano culture in Texas was inherited from the Spanish settlers and Spanish-colonized indigenous communities, as well as immigrants who settled in the area before it became part of the United States. Cattle ranchers, emerging from Spanish influence, gave rise to the term "cowboys."

Symbols of the United States and Canada

The U.S. flag's 13 stripes represent the original 13 colonies. The flag now has 50 stars, for the current 50 states, but it had 13 stars when first created in 1777. Canadian Olympic athletes were the first to wear the recognizable single red maple leaf on a white field in 1904. However, this symbol didn't officially become part of Canada's flag until 1965.

The American bald eagle, unique to North America, was chosen as the U.S. symbol for its majesty and independence. The beaver, whose richly furred pelt first drove Europe's interest in North America and its fur trade, is the historic national symbol of Canada.

The queen of England, Elizabeth II, is still considered the queen of Canada and is featured prominently on the country's currency.

Members of Canada's national police force, the Mounties, are formally called the Royal Canadian Mounted Police. The recognizable Mounties have taken on symbolic importance in the Canadian national identity.

Individualism is a trait valued in both the United States and Canada, influenced by the explorers, cowboys, and settlers who ventured away from their homes and into the unknown throughout their history. The United States especially values independence, as reflected in cultural icons such as the Liberty Bell and the Statue of Liberty and in the words of its Declaration of Independence, Pledge of Allegiance, national anthem, and Bill of Rights.

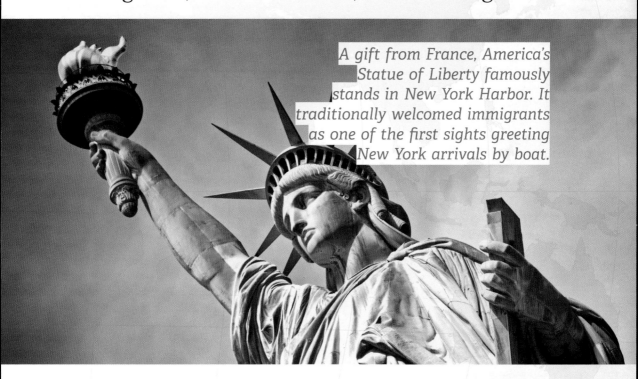

A gift from France, America's Statue of Liberty famously stands in New York Harbor. It traditionally welcomed immigrants as one of the first sights greeting New York arrivals by boat.

individualism: Doctrine that the interests of the individual are or ought to be most important; also conduct guided by such a doctrine.

3

MELTING POTS, MOSAICS, AND MUSIC

O ver the years, U.S. and Canadian **immigration** has occurred in waves. Each group faced difficult obstacles. In the 19th century, Chinese and European Catholic and Jewish immigrants faced social persecution. Today, Latin American, Asian, and Middle Eastern immigrants and refugees, among others, deal with racism and legal hurdles. Each of these immigrant groups has also contributed to U.S. and Canadian cultures with their labor, art, and the culture they brought with them.

CULTURAL CONNECTIONS

The banjo, most associated with country and folk music, was created by enslaved Africans and their descendants, who added elements of the European guitar to traditional African gourd instruments.

immigration: The act of coming to a country to settle there.

The Traveling Fiddle

European immigrants brought their music and instruments with them. The first known fiddle on American soil dates to 1620, and up until about 1960, fiddles were the instruments of choice for dance music in rural Canada.

Celtic fiddle tunes were a key building block of modern country and folk music. In the Appalachian region of the United States, Irish and Scottish traditional music blended with African American blues and hymns to become bluegrass.

Displaced Acadians brought their French ballads and fiddle music from Canada to the American South, where—influenced by the music of their new neighbors, Caribbean freed slaves, Native Americans, Spanish colonists, and Anglo-Americans—Cajun music developed as a distinct genre of its own.

On Cape Breton Island, Nova Scotia, the world's largest fiddle stands as a 60-foot-tall (18.3 m) tribute to the area's famous fiddling, which originated in the traditional music style brought by Scottish immigrants.

In 1908, Jewish playwright Israel Zangwill wrote a play titled *The Melting Pot*. In 1922, travel writer Victoria Hayward first described Canada as a **mosaic**. These ideas came from ways of thinking about immigration—one about assimilation and one about **multiculturalism**. In the melting pot concept, all immigrants join and become part of a common culture. In the mosaic idea, the separate identities of immigrants continue to exist separately, side by side but also part of one beautiful whole. In recent years, a "salad bowl" concept has been used in the United States. Like the Canadian mosaic, this perspective views the cultures as part of a whole while still maintaining their original identity.

CULTURAL CONNECTIONS

Japanese sushi increased in popularity in North America after the invention of the California roll, which includes avocado. However, both Vancouver, Canada, and Los Angeles, California, claim credit for creating this food fusion!

mosaic: Something made up of different things that fit together to form a pattern

Multiculturalism can be seen in musical **genres** born in the United States. Southern gospel music, blues, and jazz originated within black communities, primarily in the South. In rural communities, working-class whites and blacks living as neighbors picked up each other's work music, leading to combinations that became bluegrass and country. Expanding urban centers that brought diverse people closer and radio stations playing different music styles led to the fusion of rhythm and blues,

Musician Elvis Presley didn't invent rock and roll, but he made it massively popular. Elvis introduced a white audience to styles that black artists were already playing.

Rap group N.W.A is pictured on its tour for Straight Outta Compton, *the 1988 album credited with redefining hip-hop by including rap lyrics about gangster life in inner-city America.*

multiculturalism: The preservation of different cultures or cultural identities within a unified society.

Immigrant-Created Cuisine

Spaghetti and meatballs is a combination rarely found in Italy, but it's long been a staple of Italian American cuisine. Corned beef and cabbage is considered an Irish dish, but bacon and cabbage was the more popular combination in Ireland. Immigrants escaping the Irish potato famine could afford meat in America—specifically, Jewish corned beef from neighboring Eastern European immigrants.

Immigrants didn't just introduce their country's foods, such as Hungarian goulash or the Greek gyro, to North America. Substitutions when ingredients weren't available and an inspiration to sell to a new market caused immigrants to design and refine entirely new dishes. Ongoing fusion of food styles continues to this day.

Poutine—french fries and cheese curds covered in gravy—originated in Quebec and has became a common Canadian food. "Poutine" comes from Québécois slang meaning "mess."

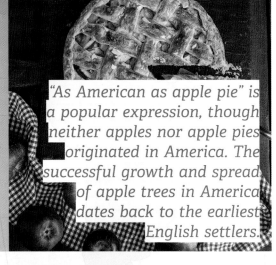

"As American as apple pie" is a popular expression, though neither apples nor apple pies originated in America. The successful growth and spread of apple trees in America dates back to the earliest English settlers.

country, and jazz into rock and roll. Hip-hop and rap music developed more recently, in the 1970s, among inner-city black and Latino communities.

Even before the internet, radio waves crossed the international border. The physical closeness of the United States and Canada— in addition to their friendly border-crossing agreements—allows artists to tour both countries or spend time across the border. Music has long spread and grown between the two nations. While the United States is better known for pioneering new music genres, Canadian artists have achieved success and fame across

The American-style burgers of fast-food chain McDonald's can be found across the globe, and its Golden Arches are often seen as an example of peaceful **globalization***.*

musical genres. Some Canadian stars are Joni Mitchell and Neil Young in folk music, Celine Dion and Justin Bieber in pop, Shania Twain in country, and Drake in hip-hop.

4 HOLIDAYS AND RELIGION

As multicultural societies, the United States and Canada celebrate holidays recognized in other countries as well as holidays unique to them. Both nations celebrate religious and nonreligious holidays, but while the United States and Canada are largely made up of Christian citizens, neither has an official religion. Almost every religion in the world can be found within these countries, and all are supposed to be equal under the law. The United States federally recognizes 10 holidays as days off work, including Martin Luther King Jr. Day, honoring the civil rights leader who fought against black **segregation** and **discrimination**. Canada recognizes five nationwide holidays.

American Independence Day is celebrated on July 4 every year with grand firework displays and large parades. This photo shows one of the country's largest firework displays in New York City.

U.S. states and Canadian provinces can choose additional holidays, such as Texas Independence Day or Islander Day in Prince Edward Island.

July 4, often marked with fireworks, celebrates American independence. July 1, similarly, is Canada Day, celebrating when the former colonies became a unified nation. Thanksgiving, originating as a celebration of the autumn harvest, occurs in both United States and Canada, but in different months. Canadian Thanksgiving takes place in October. On the same day, Americans observe Columbus Day to celebrate Christopher Columbus's arrival in the Americas.

The U.S. holiday season begins with American Thanksgiving at the end of November, marked in New York City with a parade featuring many performances and

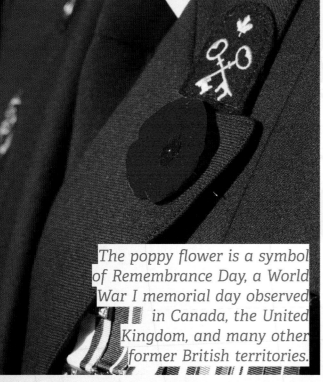

The poppy flower is a symbol of Remembrance Day, a World War I memorial day observed in Canada, the United Kingdom, and many other former British territories.

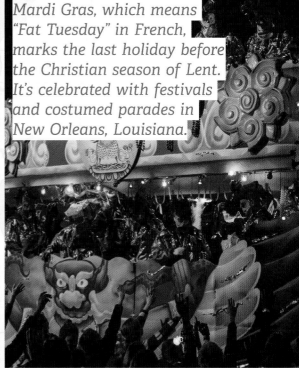

Mardi Gras, which means "Fat Tuesday" in French, marks the last holiday before the Christian season of Lent. It's celebrated with festivals and costumed parades in New Orleans, Louisiana.

floats. The Christian holiday of Christmas is celebrated on December 25 in both countries. This isn't just a religious event—more than 80 percent of non-Christians in America also celebrate Christmas. Giving and receiving gifts and spending time with family are closely associated with the celebration of Christmas in both countries. This is also true for the Jewish holiday of Hanukkah, which also occurs around the same time each year. Boxing Day, the day after Christmas, is also a holiday in Canada, as is New Year's Day in both

The Other Memorial Day

Most Canadians know July 1 as Canada Day. In the provinces of Newfoundland and Labrador, however, July 1 is also Memorial Day. During World War I, the former British colony of Newfoundland governed itself and wasn't yet part of Canada. Like the United States and Canada, Newfoundland joined the British and French as allies. On July 1, 1916, nearly 800 Newfoundlanders went into battle. Only 68 men could answer roll call the next day—the rest were all killed, wounded, or missing. Newfoundland's losses and debts from World War I ultimately led to it joining Canada. Amid the national celebration, Newfoundland still pauses to remember its soldiers' sacrifices.

countries. Hispanic, Latino, and Puerto Rican communities also celebrate Three Kings' Day on January 6.

Coca-Cola advertisements in the 1920s and 1930s helped popularize the modern image of Santa Claus still known throughout the world today.

CULTURAL CONNECTIONS

Many of the most popular Christmas songs were written by Jewish American songwriters and composers, including "The Christmas Song," "White Christmas," "Rudolph the Red-Nosed Reindeer," and "It's the Most Wonderful Time of the Year."

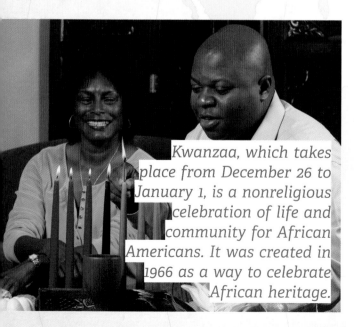

Kwanzaa, which takes place from December 26 to January 1, is a nonreligious celebration of life and community for African Americans. It was created in 1966 as a way to celebrate African heritage.

Though not days off work, the romantic Valentine's Day, Irish St. Patrick's Day, Mother's Day, and Father's Day are observed by most Canadians and Americans.

Controversial *Holidays*

As Christopher Columbus was Italian, Columbus Day celebrations were first encouraged at a time when Catholic Italian Americans were suffering from discrimination. Columbus Day continues to be a day of cultural pride and parades for some Italian American communities. In recent years, though, some U.S. states and cities have replaced Columbus Day with Indigenous Peoples' Day.

Some Southern U.S. states still hold holidays honoring the Confederacy, the union of Southern slave states that attempted to break away from the North during the U.S. Civil War. Recent **activist** movements in the United States have pushed to end these holidays, remove statues of Confederate leaders, and ban the Confederate flag, regarding them as **racist** symbols.

Pumpkin carving and children in costume going door to door to trick or treat—traditions originating in the British Isles— are common on Halloween, October 31.

Hanukkah, also known as the Festival of Lights, is a Jewish celebration commemorating the ancient dedication of the Second Temple in Jerusalem. Hanukkah typically falls in November or December and lasts eight days.

racist: Believing that that one group or race of people is better than another group or race.

5 SPORTS CULTURE

The United States has four major sports leagues. Though other professional sports leagues exist, including U.S. women's soccer and women's basketball, the "Big Four" are all men's leagues: Major League Baseball (MLB), the National Basketball Association (NBA), the National Hockey League (NHL), and the National Football League (NFL). Players in these leagues are representative of each country's diversity.

Though the leagues are primarily American, Canadian teams participate in the MLB, NBA, and NHL. Canada has its own Canadian Football League (CFL). Notably, American and Canadian football (also called gridiron) are different sports from soccer, which is called football elsewhere in the world.

Lacrosse on the Move

Lacrosse is among North America's fastest-growing sports . . . and perhaps its oldest. When Europeans arrived, early lacrosse was already played in Canada by indigenous peoples. While hockey is Canada's national winter sport, lacrosse is officially Canada's national summer sport. The Iroquois Confederacy—a native group present on both sides of the U.S.-Canada border—has the only indigenous teams from the Americas competing on an international level. Its men and women's lacrosse teams are among the top-ranked worldwide.

Five professional North American lacrosse leagues, both indoor and outdoor, now exist. Youth lacrosse participation more than doubled from 2006 to 2018, which has driven the sport's ongoing growth.

The modern sport of lacrosse, one of North America's fastest- growing sports today, has its origins in a stickball game developed by the indigenous Algonquian peoples in the Saint Lawrence Valley.

In the NFL game pictured here, the Buffalo Bills football team faces off against the Miami Dolphins. There are 32 NFL teams, spread across 30 U.S. cities, states, and regions.

Canadian and American football, which are similarly played but with rule differences, evolved from **rugby**. Baseball developed in the United States from earlier bat-and-ball sports such as the British cricket. Baseball has long been considered America's **pastime**, though football has surpassed it in popularity. Hockey comes from a stick-and-ball game that emerged in the British Isles, and indigenous peoples may have played a variation on ice even earlier. Modern ice hockey came from Canada, and ice hockey is popularly known as Canada's pastime.

pastime: An activity that someone enjoys during their free time.

The Stanley Cup, given to the annual NHL playoff champion, is the oldest professional trophy in North America and arguably the most famous sports trophy in the world.

Canadian hockey player Wayne Gretzky, known as the "Great One," is considered the best hockey player ever and still holds records for most goals, assists, and points.

Although players worldwide play professionally in the NHL, the league still has more players from Canada than any other country. Canadians spend the most money on youth sports per person in the world. Hockey, with its ice rinks, equipment, and travel costs, is an expensive athletic activity.

CULTURAL CONNECTIONS

Jim Thorpe, the first Native American to win an Olympic medal, has been called the greatest all-around athlete and American Olympian of all time. He played professional basketball, baseball, and football.

Millions of U.S. children play Little League baseball and softball. The first organized youth sports program in the world and still the world's largest today, Little League is now in 80 countries worldwide.

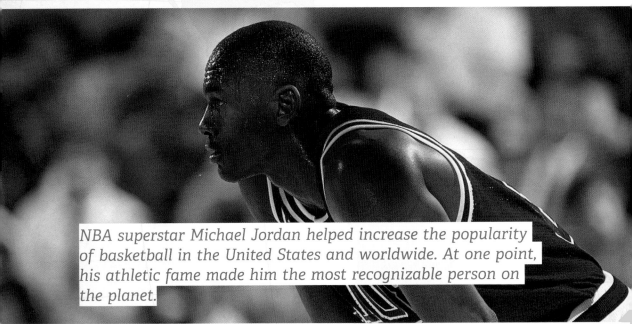

NBA superstar Michael Jordan helped increase the popularity of basketball in the United States and worldwide. At one point, his athletic fame made him the most recognizable person on the planet.

Though it was invented in the United States and widely played in schools, youth groups, and semiprofessional leagues, basketball only began catching up to baseball and football after cable television spread during the 1980s. Watching sporting events on TV has become as much a part of North American culture as attending them. The NFL Super Bowl championship is the most-watched annual sporting event and television program in the United States and frequently the most-watched in Canada as well.

Olympic Accomplishments

In the athletic competition between the world's nations, the United States has earned more total Summer Olympic medals than any other country. At Summer Games, U.S. athletes have dominated most at track and field events, swimming, shooting, and boxing. At the Winter Olympics, U.S. athletes have medaled most often at speed skating, alpine and freestyle skiing, and snowboarding. Snowboarding as a sport developed in the United States.

The less **populous** Canada ranks behind the United States in total medals. The Winter Olympics is Canada's stronger season—Canada leads the world in gold medals in ice hockey, freestyle skiing, and curling. The most-watched television event in Canadian history was Canada's 2010 gold medal-winning Olympics Final hockey game against Team USA.

Most professional players come from college teams. Though the practice is more prominent in the United States, colleges and universities in both countries offer athletic scholarships to attract student athletes. Participating in school sports and **recreational** youth leagues, such as Little League baseball, is part of growing up in America, for girls as well as boys.

6

CULTURAL DIFFUSION AND THE CINEMATIC WORLD

The English language being forced on indigenous North American peoples, German Christmas trees becoming a holiday tradition, American fast-food chains opening worldwide: all of these are examples of **cultural diffusion**.

CULTURAL CONNECTIONS

Canada's best-known fast food chain, coffee and doughnut shop Tim Hortons, is named for a hockey player and has locations in Europe, the Middle East, Asia, and 12 U.S. states.

cultural diffusion: The process of spreading cultural traits from one region to another.

Diffusion occurs regularly between the United States and Canada, with sports and music spreading freely between the two close countries. Books, such as American classic *Little Women* and Canadian classic *Anne of Green Gables*, gave global readers a picture of what it was like to come of age in these countries. Recordings, from old vinyl records to modern streaming services, contribute to new music genres spreading worldwide. In turn, bands from other countries, such as the British Beatles and Rolling Stones, started playing these styles and becoming popular in North America.

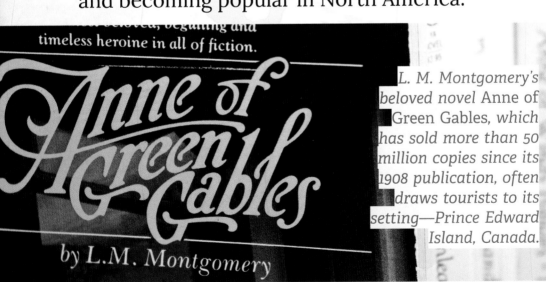

timeless heroine in all of fiction.

Anne of Green Gables

by L.M. Montgomery

L. M. Montgomery's beloved novel Anne of Green Gables, which has sold more than 50 million copies since its 1908 publication, often draws tourists to its setting—Prince Edward Island, Canada.

The American Superhero

Comic books became a major aspect of U.S. pop culture with the first appearance of Superman in 1938. Cocreators Jerry Siegel, an American, and Joe Shuster, a Canadian American, were both sons of Jewish immigrants. They came up with an idea for a super-strong immigrant from the planet Krypton, who stood for "truth, justice, and the American way."

In 1940, Superman's first **adaptation** outside comics premiered as a radio broadcast. American superhero comics were used to promote American involvement in World War II. Along with Superman, Wonder Woman and Captain America—both with costumes inspired by the American flag—became recognizable as popular American symbols worldwide through comics and their adaptations. Comic book conventions for fans, begun in New York City, now take place globally.

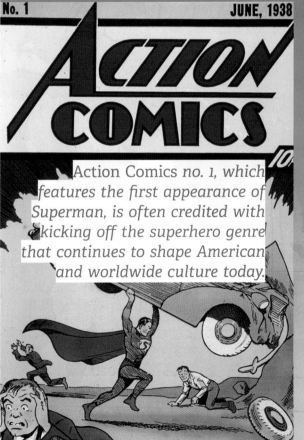

Action Comics no. 1, which features the first appearance of Superman, is often credited with kicking off the superhero genre that continues to shape American and worldwide culture today.

The American film industry–based in Hollywood, California–has played a tremendous role in spreading ideas of American culture worldwide. Since the early 20th century, the United States has been the major producer of motion pictures, with other countries importing Hollywood products. Movie versions of musicals, performed as live theater on Broadway in New York City, and movies starring Elvis Presley and his rock and roll, helped spread other American contributions to world culture.

The Hollywood sign, originally erected to advertise a real estate development in the 1920s, has become an enduring symbol of the glitz and glamour of the U.S. film industry.

Times Square, with its dazzling displays of Broadway plays, attracts millions of visitors to the theater district of New York annually.

Canada has a thriving independent film industry, including **francophone** films. Nonetheless, Canadian **cinema** is closely tied to the U.S. industry. Canadian actors, writers, and directors work in Hollywood. American movies film in Canada and vice versa. Popular American television series, such as *Grey's Anatomy* and shows on the CW Network, film in the Canadian city of Vancouver. Both Toronto and Vancouver have been called "Hollywood North" because of the areas' increasing role in creating popular television series.

Welcome to Walmart

How far to the nearest Walmart? Incredibly, most Americans live within 15 miles (24.1 km) of a Walmart, the world's largest **retail** chain. Beginning with one store location opened by Sam Walton in Arkansas in 1962, Walmart expanded outward in rural and suburban areas. Big-box stores like Walmart meant shoppers didn't have to drive as far to a city or mall. Small stores have struggled to match these chains' low prices.

Walmart has spread to all parts of Canada except the Arctic territory of Nunavut, where the majority population is Inuit. Online shopping, especially on Amazon, is Walmart's major competition worldwide.

The U.S. sitcom Friends continues to be one of the most popular television shows, even more than a decade after it last aired. Viewers worldwide have used it to try to learn English.

Many modern immigrants first experienced American culture and learned or improved their English from U.S.-made cinema, now even more readily available through online streaming. In the internet age, English is a dominant language—but nearly every language

CULTURAL CONNECTIONS

The same man created the second- and third-highest-earning Hollywood films of all time. *Avatar* and *Titanic* were both made by Canadian writer and director James Cameron.

Blue jeans, today one of the world's most popular articles of clothing, developed out of pants originally made for miners. Levi Strauss and Co.'s 501 style, introduced in 1890, is an icon of American fashion.

in the world can be found digitally, with content in other languages growing as more users get online. How to include primarily oral (not written) indigenous languages online remains unclear, but new technology is always providing new opportunities for advancing translation tools, connecting speakers of endangered languages, and making teaching material readily accessible. Like both the United States and Canada, the new digital world is a multicultural society.

GLOSSARY

activist: One who acts strongly in support of or against an issue or cause; a person who uses or supports strong actions to help make changes in politics or society.

adaptation: Something that is rewritten into a new form.

cinema: Movies, especially the film industry.

conical: Having a shape similar to a cone, with one pointed end and one circular end.

discrimination: Unfair treatment of people because of their race or beliefs.

domesticate: To adapt (a plant or animal) from a natural state for human use.

genre: A type or style of music or other artistic content.

immigrant: One who comes to a country to settle there.

nomadic: Having to do with people who move from place to place.

populous: Having a lot of people living in a place.

rugby: A ball-based game on which American football is based.

segregation: The forced separation of races or classes.

tundra: Cold northern lands that lack forests and have permanently frozen soil below the surface.

INDEX

FOR MORE INFORMATION

BOOKS:

Baker, Brynn. *Life in America: Comparing Immigrant Experiences*. North Mankato, MN: Capstone Press, 2016.

Corrigan, Kathleen. *Canada Through Time: First Nations and Early Explorers*. North Mankato, MN: Read Me, 2016.

Lawton, Cassie M., and Raymond Bial. *The People and Culture of the Shoshone*. New York, NY: Cavendish Square, 2017.

WEBSITES:

National Geographic Kids

kids.nationalgeographic.com

This website, designed for kids by National Geographic, includes culture information and facts, particularly on the U.S. states and Native Americans.

The Canadian Encyclopedia

www.thecanadianencyclopedia.ca/en

The online version of Canada's national encyclopedia provides insight on worldwide topics from a uniquely Canadian perspective and in a highly readable format.

Google Arts and Culture

artsandculture.google.com/

This website is available through Google's partnership with museums. Stories on the United States and Canada include high-quality photos, providing visitors an opportunity to view art exhibits and take a virtual tour of landmarks.